Let's Try Runes

A Taster Guide for Beginners

Ann J. Clark

Ann J. Clark

First edition published in the UK December 2018

Published by Calico Cat Press

Contents

Ann J. Clark

Introduction

The first time I encountered runes it was in J.R.R. Tolkien's *The Hobbit*, with its treasure map covered in dwarf runes and the handy rune-to-English translation guide in the Author's Notes. I spent the summer writing secret messages in runes and it wasn't until several years later that I discovered that runes existed outside of fiction and had, in fact, been around for centuries.

The modern resurgence of runes owes as much to fictional works that draw on Norse history and mythology as it does to the rune-casters and occultists who revived it for use in their workings, and whichever way you've come to the runes, there's no doubt that they're a fascinating subject to explore.

Runes were used as both an ancient alphabet to communicate in daily life, and as a divination tool to communicate with the more esoteric world of gods, spirits and natural energies, so clearly they have been, and still are, a useful method to relay information.

As you'll see from the history section, the rune alphabet has evolved and changed depending on where and when it was used – this taster guide focusses on the Elder Futhark set of runes – the standard twenty-four runes that are the most popular variation used for divination; but whether you only want to experiment with rune divination or want to begin a deeper rune-based spiritual exploration, our main aim with this guide is to give you the foundation skills of modern rune craft: what runes are, how to make them, how to use them, and a start for understanding what they mean. We hope you can take these skills and use them as a basis for your future journeys with runes.

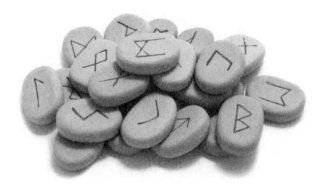

Brief History

I know that I hung on a windy tree
nine long nights,
wounded with a spear, dedicated to Odin,
myself to myself,
on that tree of which no man knows from where its
roots run.

No bread did they give me nor a drink from a horn,
downwards I peered;
I took up the runes,
screaming I took them,
then I fell back from there.

-The Poetic Edda

The story goes that once upon a long ago, the
great god Odin sought knowledge of runes and
their power and so hung himself from the
legendary world-tree Yggdrasil. They say he
hung there for nine nights and nine days,
without food or water or aid, impaled on his
own spear as a sacrifice to himself; and when he
saw the runes below him, his sacrifice
rewarded, he fell. He then took up the runes

and rose up in understanding of them and their power, and so had command of the magic of the world. This knowledge he would later pass onto mankind.

The story of Odin's initiation as the first rune-master can be found in *The Poetic Edda* – a book of Old Norse minstrel poems that were shared orally between bards for centuries until they were collected and written down in book form, possibly around the 1200's AD. Opinion is divided about when the original poems were composed – historians popularly estimate the range between 800 -1100 AD, though earlier dates have also been suggested, but we have evidence that the runic alphabet and use of runes for divination date earlier than that.

Pre-dating the *Poetic Edda* by several centuries, there are tales of the use of runes for spiritual, divination or magical purposes being recorded at least as far back as 98 BC with the Roman historian Tacitus, who stated of the ancient Germanic people - "For divination and the casting of lots they have the highest possible regard. Their procedure in casting lots is uniform. They break off a branch of a fruit tree and slice it into strips; they mark these by certain signs and throw them, as random chance will have it, onto a white cloth." While we do not know for certain what signs were marked on these wood strips, it is popularly thought they there were an early form of the runes.

Archaeological evidence shows that runes were used as an alphabet by the Germanic peoples from around 100 or 200 AD, then were carried through migration and trade from the Germanic regions to Scandinavia and other European regions. Artefacts such as jewellery, tools, weapons, amulets and rune stones have been found with rune inscriptions in places ranging from Schleswig in North Germany to Fyn, Sjælland and Jylland in Denmark, and Skåne in Sweden, while the Einang runestone in Oppland, Norway, has been dated to around 300 AD.

As the runes travelled, their number changed to accommodate the words, sounds and spelling used by local dialects – the oldest and core version of the runic alphabet is the twenty-four rune Elder Futhark – so called because the first six runes – Fehu, Uruz,

Ann J. Clark

Thurisaz, Ansuz, Raidho and Kenaz – spell
Futhark!

Around 400 AD, when the runes travelled
to Frisia (the Netherlands) and England, the
runic alphabet gained letters (going up to
twenty-six or thirty-three depending on region,
time and sources) and became known as the
Anglo-Saxon Futhark; meanwhile the Younger
Futhark developed in around 800 AD in the
Scandinavian regions and lost letters, taking the
Younger Futhark down to sixteen letters. The
Younger Futhark then later evolved in
Scandinavia to a twenty-six letter version called
Medieval runes in 1100 AD, and then in the
Dalarna region of Sweden, the Medieval rune
form then further evolved into Dalecarlian
runes in 1500 AD.

The runes' use in divination can be seen
in literature from the late 1200's in the *Saga of
Erik the Red*, which describes a seer who is
popularly assumed to be a rune-mistress as

"about her waist she had a linked charm belt with a large purse. In it she kept the charms which she needed for her predictions," and in the *Poetic* and *Prose Eddas*, many references to rune divination can be found.

The increase of Christianisation saw the decline of rune use and the 1600's saw attempts to ban the use of runes in Iceland due to the Church's opinion of connections between runic writing and witchcraft, with some people recorded as burnt to death for possession of rune staves; however in Sweden at the same time, there was an attempt by Johannes Bureus to make runes the official alphabet of Sweden and runic calendars are reputed to have still been in use in areas of Sweden up until the late 1800's.

Knowledge of how to use runes for divination was lost somewhere in this period, as rune-lore was passed orally so no written records of how to cast or what divinatory meanings were assigned each rune are known to exist; but what we do have are records of the poems used by Norsemen to help them recall the meanings of each letter of the alphabet – first recorded by George Hickes in 1705 then later reproduced in A.E. Farnham's *A Sourcebook of the History of the English*, the rune poems give the name and general concept behind each sound/letter, and this has become a significant contributor to the interpretation of modern rune divination.

But that alone would not give the depth of understanding that modern rune-casters need from their runes in divination or other rune related practices, so despite the runes' Germanic origins and their connections to other regions of Europe, modern rune divination also incorporates Norse mythology and history in its layers of meaning for each rune.

The Norsemen believed that carving the runes was, in itself, an act embodied with magical power, and apart from divination, also used runes to invoke higher powers or the individual qualities/energies associated with the rune. This practice has endured in modern rune use and while you can use runes to get guidance on issues, divine trends for the day or simply offer insight on an event, you can also use runes as talismans to draw certain energies to you or protect you. Once you dig into the rich symbolism behind each rune, you'll find all kinds of possibilities opening up to you for their use. But as this guide is focussed on rune divination, we'll leave it up to you to explore the other rune possibilities!

How Does It Work?

Rune-casters mix the basic runic alphabet meanings, as found in the traditional rune poems, with their own intuitive understanding on how it can be extended or applied to the situation they're enquiring about; then they add context by looking at what runes are drawn with it, and where the rune falls in the casting pattern they have chosen.

For instance: Gebo is known as the rune of gifts, but Norse traditions require returning a gift with gift so the rune can mean both generosity and equal exchange. Depending on the

Gebo

situation and surrounding runes it can also mean favours, love, equal or unequal partnerships, being aware of your own value, giving too much of yourself, receiving help, or not receiving proper appreciation for your efforts. Then when you apply it to the context of a casting, it could mean that a current issue was caused by giving too much of yourself, or that the future holds the possibility of help or favours being given to you.

The deeper your studies go into intuitive reading of runes, the more layers of each rune's qualities will be revealed, and the easier it will be for you to work out which facet of the rune's meanings are applicable to your reading; but at the most basic level, you can stick with the symbolisms and interpretation keywords we've provided in the **Interpretations** section.

Runestone in Skansen, Stockholm, Sweden

Ann J. Clark

Before You Cast Runes

The Runes

First you will need a set of runes! While many people find it easier to tune into their runes if they're made of specific wood or stones, the key thing to remember is you don't need to get fancy or expensive with your runes – just go with what is most comfortable to handle and works best for you.

You can buy runes made of stone, wood, plastic, ceramic or illustrated rune oracle cards from occult stores or online retailers. If you can't afford to buy runes, it's easy to make your own set from baked modelling clay, small stones, poker counters, plastic discs from old board games, coins of the same size, cut up card or a chopped up small branch! So long as you have twenty-four (or twenty-five if you want to use a blank rune) pieces roughly the same shape, all you need to do is carve, burn, draw, paint or stick the rune symbols on and you're good to go!

Ann J. Clark

The Rune Symbols

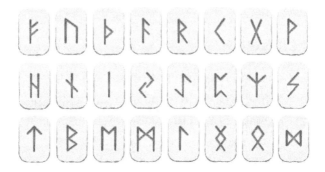

The Blank Rune

You'll find that some bought rune sets include a blank rune – opinions are divided over their use with some rune diviners finding the blank rune useful for indicating matters best left to fate, while others believing that the historical evidence doesn't support the inclusion of a blank rune and consider it to be a modern invention that doesn't add anything to an already revealing collection of symbols. Whether you incorporate it into your readings is entirely your choice, and if you find the blank rune has resonance for you then don't hesitate in using it. You'll find interpretation keywords for the blank rune, as with the other runes, in the **Interpretations** section.

Rune Bag

If your rune set doesn't already come with a
bag, cloth bags in various styles and sizes can
be easily bought or made, according to your
taste and skill levels. The bag's use is two-fold
– it keeps your runes together, clean and safe,
and it can also be used to draw runes out of.
The key thing is that the bag is big enough to
get your hand in. And if you aren't able to buy,
make or otherwise acquire a cloth bag, then it's
perfectly acceptable to keep your runes in
something like a zip-lock bag.

Rune Cloth

Depending on the castings you choose to use,
you may want to acquire a cloth to cast your
runes on. A rune cloth, at its most basic, is
simply a piece of material used to cover your
table surface and form a barrier between your
divination and your furniture, increasing your
ability to keep your runes clean both physically
and psychically! You will need a cloth that's at
least 30cm x 30cm – a bandana or square scarf
will work just as well as a custom-made cloth or
something fancier. If you don't use a cloth, you

can make a casting board instead by taking a large piece of paper or card and drawing a circle or selection of answers on it. (See the **Castings** section later for more information on casting boards.)

Always remember that you don't need your runes, cloth, bag or anything else to be a specific material or cost a lot. Work with what you have, what you can make, or what you can afford, and the runes will still communicate their wisdom to you – you just have to be open to them!

How to Cast Runes

Choose Your Question

First you'll need to work out whether you're asking the runes for general life guidance or if you have a specific question as this will impact what kind of casting you use. A general guidance request will require different answer parameters to that of a specific question, and once you know what you want to know, you'll be able to pick a casting to suit!

When you've worked out what it is you need from the runes, it's worthwhile to take some extra time to work on the phrasing of your question as you'll need to focus on that when you draw your runes. Some people prefer direct questions with definitive answers, others prefer more open-ended questions that serve as a prompt for insight on possible causes and effects or potential outcomes.

Like many other aspects of rune-casting, this an area where you should be led by your own personal choice and what you're most comfortable with. When you've settled on the most appropriate version of your question, or preferred way to ask for general guidance, then you're ready to choose the casting that will answer it best.

Choose Your Casting

If you've never used runes before, a daily one rune draw is recommended as an easy and useful way to familiarise yourself with the symbols and their meanings. Writing your daily draw and its meanings in a journal will also help you get to grips with the symbols, and once you have more confidence in working with individual runes, you can expand to the castings that use multiple runes.

Castings that use multiple runes and/or a casting board have the benefit of allowing you to get better context for the runes you've drawn, get more details from the rune guidance and help fine-tune the answer to the question you may have asked.

Have a look at the **Rune Castings** section for basic draw layouts and casting boards, then experiment to find out which ones work for you, and when you've got comfortable with those, feel free to adapt the castings or create your own custom casting to suit your own personal needs.

Drawing Your Runes

Once you've decided on your question and casting layout it's time to cast your runes. For the purpose of this example, the casting will be a simple one rune draw.

First you will need to relax your body and mind in order to tune into the runes and get the best results from your enquiry.

Relax your body

Take a few deep breaths and shake your hands and wrists by your sides to loosen things up a little. Try shrugging your shoulders a few times, bring them up towards your ears and then let them drop to relax the muscles. Twitch and fidget as much as you need until you're feeling calmer and more relaxed.

Open your mind

Close your eyes and let your mind drift for a few moments while your everyday thoughts settle down. When your mind is as still as you can make it, focus on the question you've worked out.

If you have a rune bag, hold the bag while focussing on the question. You can do this with your hand in the bag if you choose, as some people find it helpful to run the runes through their fingers as they think of their question. When it feels like the time is right, pick a rune from the bag.

Alternatively, if you don't have a rune bag of any kind, you could try muddling the runes on a table surface and picking one with your eyes closed.

Once you've drawn your rune, it's time to interpret it. Check out the **Interpretations** section for simple keywords and an explanation of the symbol itself. If any keywords don't feel right then feel free to discard them – let your intuition guide you towards what the rune symbol means for you at that particular time.

<u>Interpreting the Runes</u>

While you don't need a familiarity with Norse mythology to use runes, we've found that reading runes becomes a more enriching experience with the knowledge of these stories, so we recommend finding one of the many books of Norse mythology to read in your spare time!

The Aettir

The runes of the Elder Futhark are commonly divided into three sets, sometimes called Aetts. Aett is a term with multiple meanings – in Faroese it means direction or family, in Icelandic it also means family and traditionally rune-casters have assigned the meaning of eight directions or simply eight to the term, giving Aett the general meaning of family-of-eight.

Ann J. Clark

The Aett or Set of Freyja, Goddess of Fertility and Love

Fehu, Uruz, Thurisaz, Ansuz, Raidho, Kenaz, Gebo, Wunjo

These are the first eight runes and deal with themes relating to fertility, peace, love, good fortune, forging order out of chaos, creation, home and hearth, material possessions and physical matters, the road to knowledge and power.

The Aett or Set of Hagalaz (elemental force of hail and storm) or Heimdall, Watcher of the Gods

Hagalaz, Naudhiz, Isa, Jera, Eihwaz, Perdhro, Elhaz, Sowelu

These next eight runes deal with themes relating to patience, watchfulness, courage, achievements, personal growth, spiritual matters, deeper knowledge seeking, opportunities, chaos, disruptive forces that cause great change, elemental forces, and outside forces beyond our control.

The Aett or Set of Teiwaz, or Tyr, God of War and Justice

Teiwaz, Berkana, Ehwaz, Mannaz, Laguz, Inguz, Othala, Dagaz

These last eight runes deal with themes of divinity, order, justice, conflict and its resolution, the spiritual world, transformative experiences, human condition, society and social matters, mental or spiritual growth, challenges and how those challenges are dealt with.

Interpretation Keywords

Reversed Rune Meanings

As with the tarot and other divination methods, the runes can be read with different meanings if drawn upside down – all this means is that the meaning of the rune is reversed, delayed, or cast in a more negative light – reading reversed, or inverted, meanings of runes is a matter of personal choice and many rune-casters don't do it in order to keep things simpler. Again, go with the method that you're most comfortable with and if reversed readings don't work for you, then don't use them!

Fehu
Sound: "f"

Stands for: Cattle

Power and wealth, property, status, social position, career, emotional security, fulfilment of love, pregnancy, fertility, growth.

Inverted – financial loss, lack of fulfilment, sexual frustration, procreational difficulties, female health problems, weight gain problems.

Expanded:

Fehu is the rune of cattle – this means it represents ideas concerned with wealth, property and status and the work necessary to nurture or keep it, as traditionally the ownership of cattle was a sign of prosperity in the ancient world. As the first of Freyja's Set, Fehu also embodies the qualities of fertility, fulfilment of love, and growth.

Drawing Fehu suggests a need to take care of both your internal and external possessions – your emotions and personal well being, as well as your possessions and wealth. Its associations with fertility and growth can either indicate matters relating to love, fertility, pregnancy or childbirth; or can be translated as fertile times to start or grow businesses, especially creative related ones.

Ann J. Clark

Uruz

Sound: "oo"

Stands for: Auroch/wild ox

Masculinity, physical and material planes, opportunities to better self, possible financial improvement from work after using energy or strength, acquiring and controlled use of physical skills and training others in this, promotions, harnessing energy, being able to carry impossible seeming burdens, endurance, strength, overcoming obstacles, courage, patience.

Inverted - missed opportunities, misplaced power, uncontrolled strength, lack of strength – either physical or metaphorical.

Expanded:

Uruz is the rune of the wild ox, or ancient auroch – this means it represents ideas concerned with primal creative forces, strength, endurance, overcoming obstacles and courage, and is a rune often used by warriors to lend them extra strength in battle as it signifies the overcoming of great difficulties to reach victory.

Drawing Uruz suggests a time where burdens are being carried and challenges must be met with strength and patience before victory can be achieved. It also indicates a time of learning new physical related skills or teaching your skills to others, of harnessing your energy or someone else's energy in the right way to achieve the best result.

 ## Thurisaz
Sound: "th"

Stands for: Thorn (or Giant)

Protection – physical, mental and psychic, use of offensive deterrent, physical defences or protection from attack. Matters must run their course and not be forced, family matters may be indicated, caution and self-protection needed in decisions.

Inverted – a wrong decision, tension, introversion, misplaced power, jealousy, over-

defensive attitude, aggression used for wrong reasons.

Expanded:

Thurisaz is the rune of the thorn – this means it represents ideas concerned with protection in the physical, mental/emotional and psychic realms. It also has connections with the ancient Norse giants and the god Thor and so also concerns matters relating to aggression and challenges, especially when those challenges are directed at outmoded traditions.

Drawing Thurisaz suggests a need to look to your or someone else's protection, and that decisions or actions must be made with an element of caution. It can also mean the need to let matters run their course and not force your way through the obstacles you see, as this may cause you more harm than good.

Ansuz

Sound: "aa" as in "aah"

Stands for: Mouth (or Divine Breath)

Guidance from above, authority, superiors, ancestors, elders, parents, inheritances – material and emotional, father figures, god figures.

Inverted – blind faith, obsession, mental complexes, fanaticism, over dominant attitude, abuse of power, problems with parents or authority figures or government bodies.

Expanded:

Ansuz is the rune of the mouth or divine breath – this means it represents ideas concerned with guidance, communication and inspiration. It also has strong connections to the god Odin so incorporates his qualities of wisdom, learning, authority, elders, inheritances and people held in high esteem.

Drawing Ansuz suggests the need to give or receive advice or wisdom, and also the presence of an older person who will be helpful or influential. Ansuz also indicates a need to listen to inner guidance.

Raidho
Sound: "r"

Stands for: Wheel, Cartwheel (or Riding)

Movement, transport matters, exploration, purposeful journeys, changes, forward progress, movement in education or imagination, personal affairs moving if previously held up.

Inverted – immobility, stubbornness, lack of imagination, difficulties with travel and transport, necessary but unwanted journey or visit, unconstructive changes.

Expanded:

Raidho is the rune of the wheel or of riding – this means it represents ideas concerned with movement and transport. This can be understood literally in the realms of travel, transport and exploration; or can be more ideological with the progress of ideas or projects.

Drawing Raidho suggests a time when things are moving or changing fast after a period of staying still - though things may seem a little bumpy, so courage may be necessary to see you through to your destination.

Kenaz
Sound: "k"

Stands for: Torch

Good health, healing, lucky in love matters, improved status, success, mental illumination, burst of creativity, celebrations, social activity, becoming centre of attention.

Inverted – health problems, heart trouble, general lowering of immunity resistance, loss of valuables, feeling of blindness, lack of direction or guidance.

Ann J. Clark

Expanded:

Kenaz is the rune of the torch – this means that it represents ideas concerned with illumination and warmth in the physical, mental/emotional and psychic realms. Torches were used to kindle festival fires, forges and hearths so Kenaz also represents the ignition of things and the cleansing that fire can bring.

Drawing Kenaz suggests the illumination of new insights, creativity or knowledge, and the warmth of love with a partner, with fires of passion igniting and relationships kindling. The fire of Kenaz also has protective qualities and can indicate the efforts you have kindled will be ignited into success. This is a very positive rune to draw.

Gebo
Sound: "g" as in "gift"

Stands for: Gift

Give and take, payment for benefits or gifts received, a contract, opportunity, useful talent or gift, good partnerships, happiness in love needs cooperation and compromise from both partners.

Inverted – illness, shortcoming that needs to be accepted, loss, a swindle, pointless sacrifice, martyrdom, exploitation, personal skills not up to the task.

Expanded:

Gebo is the rune of gifts – this means that it represents ideas concerned with generosity and equal exchange, most particularly in the giving and receiving of gifts, favours, love and other beneficial emotions and acts, information, ideas or skills. As Norse traditions required that the giving of a gift be met with receiving one in return, Gebo can also concern the idea of giving too much or not receiving appropriate appreciation for actions or emotions or efforts.

Drawing Gebo suggests the need for equal partnerships, being aware of your own value, receiving due rewards, love and the need for both partners to put work and communication into the relationship to maintain it in the long term. It also indicates that help will be given if needed and that sharing your time, skills or emotions with another will be beneficial to you both.

Wunjo
Sound: "w", "v"

Stands for: Joy

Artistic or spiritual awakening, luck or gain in creative or inspirational matters, joy and emotional happiness, improved health, promising social events, marital bliss, domestic happiness, harmony, fellowship, journeys or visitors from over water, fair haired man/ masculine person.

Inverted – avoid major decisions due to emotional over-involvement, martyrdom, depression, over-emotion, bad judgement, difficulty in seeing clearly, need to wait before making decisions, problems with digestive system or body fluids or female hormonal balance or menstrual cycle.

Expanded:

Wunjo is the rune of joy – this means that it represents ideas concerned with personal and shared happiness, success, luck and recognising blessings.

Drawing Wunjo suggests a time where good news or good events are on the horizon – the joyful results can occur in any area of your life but are more likely in matters that echo the Viking idea of happiness which includes being accepted as part of an extended family and having enough wealth, shelter and food – so look to domestic matters and family and friends first, as Wunjo indicates shared fellowship with shared concerns and good fortune. That said, also look to your own personal happiness as Wunjo also represents the happiness, success, and recognition of worth you've attained through your own efforts.

Hagalaz

Sound: "h"

Stands for: Hail, Hailstone

Opportunity to rebuild better after destruction, natural disaster, sudden twist in fate, havoc, disruption of plans, unforeseen events, family sickness, unexpected births, be prepared for the unexpected, good events that turn world upside down.

Inverted – Disruptions, delay, deserved disaster, accidents, possible death if other ruins near emphasize it.

Expanded:

Hagalaz is the rune of hail or hailstones – this means that it represents ideas concerned with elemental forces, sudden violent changes, natural disasters or unexpected twists of fate. In Norse mythology it was believed that ice and fire were the two primal forces of creation so Hagalaz also embodies the cosmic seed that comes before life is ignited by the flame of the Kenaz rune.

Drawing Hagalaz suggests a sudden or unwelcome change must be endured to achieve a result that transforms sorrow to happiness. It indicates delays and interference from outside forces you have no influence over and suggests using this as an opportunity to learn and grow from your current circumstances as these delays, changes, or interference are necessary to your long term progress and will provide the foundation for the future.

Naudhiz
Sound: "n"

Stands for: Necessity (or Need)

Need for patience and restraint, self-preservation, necessity, instinctive needs, creative needs, basic requirements from job or relationship, need to eat, need to protect family, need to support oneself, motivating force.

Inverted – inability to let go, immobility, muscular strain and stress, mental problems, bottled up feelings, physical tension, emotional tightness, a personality who is greedy or envious or cautious and hard to get along with.

Ann J. Clark

Expanded:

Naudhiz is the rune of need or necessity – this means that it represents ideas connected with the needs that drive you to action and the necessities of life and survival.

Drawing Naudhiz suggests a time to be aware of your needs and see that you work to fulfil them – Naudhiz indicates the ambition needed to motivate you in your career aims or other potential achievements, and also feeds the passion that manifests in a relationship with someone you desire. However, Naudhiz also warns of tempering your flames so that you don't burn out of control and destroy what you need – your emotions may be high or your mind not as clear as it could be, so try to acknowledge and understand current limitations as these limitations may be necessary boundaries that will shape your future progress. Above all, think before you act and don't do anything now that will impinge on the future stability of you or your family.

Isa

Sound: "i", "ee" as in "east"

Stands for: Ice

Feeling of immobilisation, patience needed before success can be achieved, impediment, obstacle, stopped plans, frozen money, nothing good from present situation, things must be postponed. Frozen feelings, emotional detachment.

*Due to its unique appearance, there is a school of thought that suggests Isa is the only rune without a reversed meaning. If you want to use reversed meanings with Isa, then you'll need to put a small mark on the edge you want to assign as the bottom of the rune!

Inverted – stubbornness, refusal to be moved or adapt, mental paralysis, no clear or constructive ideas, immobility, fear, coldness, avoidance. Physical impediments like rheumatism, arthritis or paralysis.

Expanded:

Isa is the rune of ice – this means that it represents ideas connected with a necessary freeze in activity so that things can be postponed and future events or activities prepared for.

Drawing Isa suggests a time where progress is slow and that the desired result must be delayed for your own benefit. There could be a cooling off in a relationship or business partnership, or even a separation of some sort, but this is likely be temporary and may change given time. Patience is the keyword for financial and emotional matters, and it's better to leave things to work themselves out as pushing for results will not end well.

Jera

Sound: "j" like the "y" in "year"

Stands for: Harvest (or Year or Season)

Time for a fresh start, wheel of fortune, new projects, contracts signed, change of home, debts paid, end of a cycle, time of expectation, promise of fulfilment, possible waiting period before beneficial change occurs, rewards for work done or time/energy invested.

Inverted – longer waiting period, missed opportunities, resistance to change, inability to recognise opportunities or advantages of a situation.

Expanded:

Jera is the rune of harvest – this means it represents ideas concerned with the harvest and the turning of seasons.

Drawing Jera indicates that it is time to receive the rewards of your work, time, or energy, that projects are coming to fruition and that things you have been patiently waiting for are about to occur. It also indicates the beginning of new things, and fertility leading to something that will need to be nurtured for it to thrive.

Eihwaz

Sound: "eo", "æ"

Stands for: Yew Tree

Thinking outside of the box, avoiding difficulty, flexible approach, use others strength against them, manipulation of others power and dominance, adapting to new and different situations, taking one step back to move two steps forward, pitfalls avoided, inconvenient situations turn out advantageous.

Inverted – refusal to face up to problems, escapism, deviousness, craftiness, indecision, vacillation, step back in progress, withdrawal, relapse into mental or physical illness.

Expanded:

Eihwaz is the rune of the yew tree – this means it represents ideas concerned with natural endings and new beginnings, as the yew tree was considered to be the longest living tree and was associated with longevity and eternal life. The yew tree was also considered to be sacred to the Norse god Ullr, a hunter god of winter and archery who was said to live in 'Yew Dales' and possibly had a bow made of yew wood. This association gives Eihwaz the qualities of flexible thinking and the need to adapt to situations.

Drawing Eihwaz suggests a time of changes, which, while less shocking or sudden than those found with Hagalaz, will be just as unwelcome, and just as beneficial once they've been endured. Eihwaz indicates the need to have a flexible attitude to your problems and be able to let go of worn out things or situations. It's a time to move on and begin new things, though the new may well be connected to the old as continuity and regeneration is a staple quality of the yew tree.

Perdhro

Sound: "p"

Stands for: The secret rune

Unexpected benefits, something not revealed yet, information or knowledge will be given at the right time, unexpected good events, luck, gain, favours which were forgotten will be

Ann J. Clark

returned. Spirit world, psychism, dreams, visions, trance-like states which may reveal prophecy.

Inverted – lack of communication, subconscious fears, phobias, deeply hidden psychosis, going behind someone's back, imaginary fears, disappointment over an expectation, favours not returned.

Expanded:

Perdhro is the rune of secrets and the unseen – this means it represents ideas concerned with things unknown or yet to be revealed, and the essential inner self. As gambling and divination were considered to be close cousins by the early Northern peoples, Perdhro also concerns matters of chance, especially chance where the querent actively works to improve their own odds, and it was believed by the Vikings that testing your luck, in both lot-casting and the real world, was a way to discover essential truths about yourself.

Drawing Perdhro suggests a time of warmth, friendships and comforts, with money coming from unexpected places and good times well starred so surprise parties or other as yet unknown celebrations may be on the horizon. Perdhro also indicates a time of inner transformation and the seeking of knowledge - dreams may be prophetic, there may be a greater interest in esoteric or hidden knowledge, memories and problem solving may also be important, and it will be necessary to look past the surface to understand the truth of a situation.

Elhaz/Algiz
Sound: "zz" as in "buzz"

Stands for: Elk, or hand held up in greeting

Creative talent, poetry, artistry, self-expression and art of their own sake, hobbies, cultural interests, study for pleasure, being part of a special interest group, duality, need for care in approaching important matters, warnings of attack or defence.

Inverted – people to avoid such as groups engaged in dodgy or illegal activities, people who are

Ann J. Clark

a bad influence, lack of creativity or self-expression, lack of opportunity to express oneself in work or life generally.

Expanded:

Elhaz, sometimes called, Algiz, has many translations and is the rune of multiple things - the elk or elk sedge or eelgrass, or sometimes a hand upraised – this means that it represents multiple ideas concerned with defence, duality of nature and creativity. The splayed hand or elk horns of the rune symbol demonstrates the capacity for defence or attack and in Old English, elk sedge was the kenning for sword, giving Elhaz the quality of a double-edged sword which can be used to harm oneself as well as others, and is more powerful than the standard blade. However, the translation of eelgrass introduces an aspect of creativity to its meaning as eelgrass was used for thatching and kindling fire but shows its double nature by also being capable of injuring those who grasp it wrong.

Drawing Elhaz suggests a time where respect and care is needed in your approach to things. Artistic matters and related careers are well-favoured and it is a good time for new creative interests. Elhaz's aspects of protection can manifest as the need to protect family and friends or yourself from hostile influences, or it could be indicative of healing, especially spiritual healing as it can suggest the need for introspection or a retreat.

Sowulo/Sowilo/Sowelu

Sound: "s"

Stands for: Sun

Fame, recognition, creative endeavour or talent being brought into the light, life force, health, healing, rest, recuperation, relaxation, hobbies, holidays, entertainment, recreational activities and interests.

Inverted – overdoing things, need for time off to relax and recharge, burnt out, muscular strain, overworked.

Expanded:

Sowelu is the rune of the sun – this means it represents ideas concerned with life, health, energy and positivity.

Drawing Sowelu suggests a time when light is entering your life – this could be love, increased spirituality, better health, better luck, new studies, more strength or vitality, a feeling of wholeness or more hope on a situation. When drawn in a reading, Sowelu improves the meanings of the runes around it, bringing extra hope and positivity to the outlook, and indicating success or victory. Sowelu also warns of overusing your energies and suggests the need to take time off to recharge so that you can harness your energy to its best use.

Teiwaz

Sound: "t"

Stands for: Creator, Tir/Tyr the war god

Anger, aggression, angst, attack, new romance which will end up explosively passionate. Activity, energy, heroism, justice, clear focus.

Inverted – lack of or misdirected energy, unrequited love, broken love affair, falling in love with the wrong person, obsessive relationship, sexual frustration, impotence, arguments, violence, damage to property. Allergies, cuts, bruises, burns, accidents, headaches.

Expanded:

Teiwaz is the rune of the god Tyr, god of war and justice - this means it represents ideas concerned with justice, battles, focus, self-sacrifice, altruism and explosive energy.

Drawing Teiwaz suggests a time where passions run high between lovers, self-sacrifice may be needed to solve a problem and opportunities must be grabbed as they will lead to success. Teiwaz also indicates a need to be aware of your resources and that of others so you can judge situations with clear thinking, develop clear aims, and follow through with a strength of purpose that allows you a straight path to your goal no matter what obstacles try and knock you off course.

Berkana

Sound: "b"

Stands for: Birch Tree (or Birch Twig)

Expansion, new beginnings, fertility, growth, ritual, familiarity, repetition, family unit, community, parties, celebrations, weddings, births.

Inverted – fatigue, lack of energy, bad news in community, ill feeling among friends, unfamiliar surroundings, sickness in family, disconcerting visits, delays, barrenness, plan not coming to fruition.

Expanded:

Berkana is the rune of the birch tree or birch twig – this means it represents ideas of birth, death and rebirth. It also has connections to multiple goddesses – Nerthus, the Great Mother; Hel, Goddess of the Underworld; and Frigg, associated with fertility and motherhood. This adds ideas of home, mothering, fertility and spirituality to Berkana.

Drawing Berkana suggests a time for new beginnings, especially those linked to the family, such as births, weddings, new jobs or homes, or events that are a cause for family celebrations. Berkana also indicates a need to nurture your own spiritual growth – now is a time to re-examine your motives and plans, and conduct an inner spring cleaning to cleanse yourself and get rid of the parts you're not happy with as this will help you reach your fullest potential.

Ehwaz

Sound: "e" as in "egg/every"

Stands for: Horse

Transport and travel. Change and methods used to create it, movement and communication, progress and method to achieve it, working animals.

Inverted – problems with transport, sick animals, immobility, handicaps, failure to get message across.

Expanded:

Ehwaz is the rune of the horse – this means it represents ideas concerned with transport and travel, movement, communication, loyalty, and harmonious relationships with people or inner and outer worlds.

Drawing Ehwaz suggests a time where harmonious partnerships full of trust and loyalty are needed, as between the horse and its rider, and the element of partnership also affects any runes drawn with it as Ehwaz reinforces the meanings of its adjacent runes.

Ehwaz's aspect of movement could indicate travel, or life changes such as a new home, new project, new job, or education journey – Ehwaz is the indicator of large-scale changes, especially concerning status, and is also a sign that emotions will be racing.

Mannaz

Sound: "m"

Stands for: Man (as in human, not gender)

Wait before making decisions, get professional advice, male or masculine person especially in authority, act with intelligence, see the bigger picture, have compassion for others, look to your connections in a community.

Inverted – Problems with those in authority, abuse of power or position, opposition from an influential person, over-strict father figure.

Ann J. Clark

Expanded:

Mannaz is the rune of humankind – this means it represents ideas concerning humanity, the strength and potential of the individual and their connection to the human race.

Drawing Mannaz suggests a need for intelligence, to see yourself or examine an issue as part of a wider pattern, accept the strengths and weaknesses of yourself and those around you, and demonstrate compassion to others. The aspect of connections highlights shared experiences and relationships, and indicates a need to be aware of both how you see yourself and how others see you. Mannaz also warns that people may not be who you think they are, and that professional advice should be sought before getting locked into anything serious. Conflicts may add to your stress but action must be carefully considered and the past may offer some insight.

Laguz

Sound: "L"

Stands for: Water (or Lake)

Intuition, the psychic realm, the sea, childbirth, change, fluidity, protection, fertility, children, the unknown.

Inverted – consult someone impartial if an issue makes you overemotional or too emotionally involved, paranoia, inability to cope with subconscious. Hormone imbalances, miscarriage, blood, menstrual or other cyclic problems, alcoholism, drug dependence, escapism.

Expanded:

Laguz is the rune of water or a lake – this means it represents ideas concerning emotions, the flow of life, the psychic realms, the tides, the sea and other bodies of water. Laguz is also associated with the Norse moon god Máni, a deity believed to have connections to the progression of time, witchcraft and divination, curses, blessings and protection for the living and the dead.

Drawing Laguz suggests a time when inner knowledge and intuition should be trusted, imagination is heightened and spiritual matters will be important. The tidal aspect of Laguz indicates an ebb and flow of emotions or events, the need to ride the currents where they take you, accept that outside forces have more control at this time, and trust that you will arrive at success in due course. Travel is also likely, particularly overseas or long distance, and may seem daunting so courage will be needed to reach the rewards at your destination.

Inguz/Ingwaz

Sound: "ng" as in "long"

Stands for: Family/fertility

Material result, fertility, production, fruition, children, completed projects, problems solved, protection, enclosure, security, staying in familiar surroundings, magic, divination, women's mysteries, problems solved if work put into them, results may be long term, friends from abroad.

Inverted – intolerance, lack of charity, non-productiveness, imprisonment, restriction, tension. Health problems related to tensions, blockages, stresses, claustrophobia, infertility.

Expanded:

Inguz is the rune of family and fertility – this means it represents ideas concerning fertility and family matters, and is another rune connected with protection, patience, and the cycle of birth, death and rebirth.

Drawing Inguz suggests a time where family matters are ascendant – new births are likely, contact with friends and family will be reinitiated, and protection of home and hearth will be on your mind. The fertility aspect of Inguz indicates a time where new beginnings and material or spiritual change is ripe, matters of creativity will be well favoured, and projects will come to fruition. This aspect can also indicate that you are in the gestation period before things bloom, so patience may be needed while you use the time to weed out any unnecessary things and give yourself a better way to blossom.

Othala

Sound: "o" as in "old"

Stands for: Home/inheritance

Money matters, documents, wills, legal matters, legacies, heirlooms, benefit through property, gifts, help from older relatives.

Inverted – physical illness, trouble with old people, theft, loss, problems with house or other physical goods.

Expanded:

Othala is the rune of home and inheritance – this means it represents ideas concerning domestic matters, the home, the family, stability, responsibilities, legacies, inheritances and duty.

Drawing Othala suggests a time where domestic matters and stability are important, possibly connected to land or property, though it can also indicate the responsibilities and customs connected with maintaining family ties and culture – marriages or engagements are likely, as are things relating to heritage or family togetherness. Othala indicates material comfort built on the continuation of generations of a family, and elders may be the source of gifts or advice, though it is possible there may be opposition due to traditional views conflicting with newer opinions. Othala also warns of the dangers of expecting things to fall into your lap – even with the benefits of inheritance or generations of family work or connections, you must still put your own effort into your aims and build on what has come before.

Dagaz
Sound: "d"

Stands for: Day

Change for the better, success, warmth, light, things in the open or easily seen, the obvious, face values, things coming to light, recognition, clarity, advertisement, image, educational success and qualification.

Inverted – things hidden or not immediately obvious, sunset, an ending, sleep, illness, coma.

Ann J. Clark

Expanded:

Dagaz is the rune of day – this means it represents ideas concerned with daylight, the light of hope, new dawns, improvements, good health, prosperity, and illumination.

Drawing Dagaz suggests a time of enlightenment and new hope, where breakthroughs will be made, answers to problems found, new attitudes or understandings will bring improvements, and you will soon transition to better times. Dagaz indicates that it is time of opportunities, ambitions to be realised, and wishes about to be fulfilled. It is also the perfect time to consider any new project or new move that seems vastly different from your usual lifestyle, and making plans for the future is advised as despite any current concerns about your own or your family's status, the future is bright!

Blank

Stands for: The karmic rune, Wyrd

Fate, destiny kismet, things decided for the querent, things known only to the gods. Look to the nearest runes to see what the fates have store.

Expanded:

The Blank Rune is the rune of fate – this means it represents ideas concerned with destiny, doom or fate.

Drawing the Blank Rune suggests a time where things are out of your control and in the hands of fate, major changes may be imminent, or a life turning point may be about to occur. If you draw this rune in a one rune casting then it also indicates that now is not the time for your question to be answered and you should leave the question for another time.

Rune Patterns

The more you read runes, the more you'll notice that certain runes have complimentary qualities, or are in opposition. You'll find that the appearance of similar runes near each other in a multi rune cast can improve or diminish the reading generally; or enhance or negate the individual runes nearest them.

Discovering the connections between runes and letting your intuition guide you to what they mean together is something you will easily learn to do, but to get started, here are a few rune patterns to look out for -

Fire and Ice Runes

According to Norse mythology, the world was created in fire and ice. In the beginning, there was just the silent and dark abyss of Ginnungagap, with Muspelheim, the realm of elemental fire on one side, and Niflheim, the realm of elemental ice on the other. Then the frost and flame from each realm crept towards each other, meeting in the abyss where the fire melted the ice and the drops formed the giant Ymir, who spawned more giants from his legs and the sweat of his armpits! The melting ice also revealed the cow Audhumla who licked the ice and uncovered the first tribe of gods. Eventually the gods slew Ymir and constructed the world from his corpse.

This gives the elements of fire and ice particular importance in the world of the runes, as without these elements, the world would not have emerged. They oppose and balance each other and their conjunction can be seen to be the necessary spark of new things.

Fire runes

Kenaz, Naudhiz, Sowelu

Drawing two or more of these runes in a reading indicates a time of intense passion, illumination and creation.

Ann J. Clark

Ice Runes

Hagalaz, Isa

Drawing both the ice runes in a reading suggests that events or required results will be extremely slow or delayed and much patience will be needed.

Fire and Ice combined

A reading that combines fire and ice runes is one where tension is indicated between the two opposing elements. Look to the specific runes to understand what shape that tension is, and remember that like the primal fire and ice of creation, their conjunction will spark the growth of something new.

Runes that increase the positivity of a reading

Sowelu, Dagaz, Kenaz, Gebo, Wunjo

When two or more of these runes are drawn together, they increase the positivity of a reading, they can bring extra hope and make a good opportunity great, a pleasant trip outstanding or family news spectacular!

Runes that speed things up

Drawing Raidho and Ehwaz together will speed up the events or results you're enquiring about.

Runes that slow things down

As previously mentioned, drawing Hagalaz and Isa together will slow down the events or results you're enquiring about.

Ann J. Clark

But as with the fire and ice runes, if you draw a slow rune with a speedy rune, there will be tension between their properties which may result in progress slowed, or delays shortened, depending on the runes around them.

Connection runes

Gebo, Wunjo, Perdhro, Berkana, Ehwaz, Mannaz, Inguz

When two or more of these runes are drawn together, it indicates that the solution, results, or events are strongly concerned with family, or a need to reach out to, or mix with, a community or partnership. Whatever the situation, connections or collaborations with other people are the key thing.

Introspection runes

Ansuz, Perdhro, Elhaz, Laguz

When two or more of these runes are drawn together, it reinforces that introspection and intuition are key.

Ann J. Clark

Rune Castings

One Rune Draw

Good for: a simple reading to learn general insight on an issue or inspiration for the day to come. Also an excellent one to use for a daily draw to gradually familiarise yourself with runes and their meanings.

How to do it: simply draw one rune from your rune bag, or muddle the runes on a table top and pick one.

Three Rune Draw #1

Good for: a simple past, present, future reading.

How to do it: draw three runes from your rune bag or muddle the runes on a table or other surface and pick 3. Lay them out in a row and interpret as follows: the first rune on the left indicates the past issues that have contributed to your current situation. The middle rune indicates your current situation or problem. The third rune indicates the possible outcome based on what has come before. As with any insight into the future, this can be changed if you recognise the factors (runes 1 and 2) that created it.

Three Rune Draw #2

Good for: suggesting a course of action for a current issue.

How to do it: draw three runes from your rune bag or muddle the runes on a table or other surface and pick three. Lay them out in a row and interpret as follows: the first rune on the left describes your current situation or question, the middle rune indicates the thing that challenges you and the third rune suggests a possible course of action to take.

Five Rune Draw

Good for: examining a current problem or issue and divining its cause, possible solution, and unseen benefits.

How to do it: Pick five runes and arrange them in a cross formation, with the first rune in the middle, the second on the left, the third above, the fourth below and the fifth to the right.

1 – Present problem or issue

2 – Past factors that contributed to problem or issue

3 – Help available for problem or issue

4 – Elements of problem or issue that need to be accepted

5 – Possible future

Sacred Grid Draw

Good for: more detailed identification of the factors that created current issues and divining possible results or directions to improve things. You'll notice that this is an extended version of the **Three Rune Draw #1**, and as such, can also be adapted to the **Three Rune Draw #2** if you require more detailed answers.

How to do it: Draw nine runes from your rune bag or pick nine runes from your pile.

Runes 1 – 3 indicate the past events that have contributed to the present issue

Runes 4 – 6 indicate the present and the factors that are keeping current issues active

Runes 7 – 9 indicate the possible future, built on the past and present, which may be changed or refined

If you prefer to read the rows of runes in a different direction, or read vertical columns instead of horizontal rows, then feel free to do that instead and find the variation you're most comfortable with!

Calendar Draw

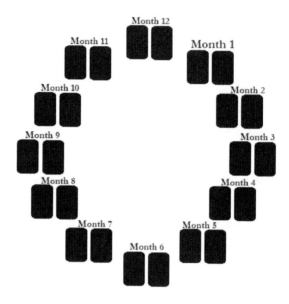

Good for: gaining insight to the months ahead.

How to do it: this one uses all twenty-four runes, so if you use the twenty-fifth blank rune, discard it for this casting.

Mix your runes up in your rune-bag or on a table top, then draw two runes. Place these

two runes at the one o'clock position in a clock face. This will be the reading for the first month. Pick another two runes and put them at the two o'clock position – this will be your reading for the second month. Continue picking out two runes and placing them around the positions in the clock face until all twenty-four runes fill all twelve positions.

Then start at month one and read the pair of runes – note how they relate to each other as well as their individual meaning. You can then continue to do this for all the following months!

If you want to try a simpler version of this casting, then only use one rune per month.

Casting Boards

Once you've got the hang of drawing runes and interpreting patterns, it's time to move on to the methods that use casting boards.

Casting boards are simply cloths, boards, or pieces of paper with areas drawn, sewn or otherwise marked on – the aim is to scatter your runes over the board and modify your interpretation of the rune by the area it falls in, and the runes it falls next to.

Basic Circle Cast

Good for: a general rune reading

How to do it: draw a large circle on a piece of paper – aim for 30cm diameter at minimum but you've got the paper, you can go up to 1m diameter for your circle. Use whichever size you can manage and feel free to experiment to find the one that works for you.

Alternatively you can make a circle using a piece of string or cord and shaping it into a circle on the floor or table.

Next draw some runes from your rune bag or rune pile. Pick between three and nine runes, depending on your own personal choice. Hold your runes in your hands, focussing on a general question, or allow your mind to drift and go blank. Then scatter the runes into the circle, much as you'd throw dice. Discard any runes that fall out of the circle, and turn any upside down runes the right way up so you can see all the rune symbols.

Next look at the runes – are there any that stand out? Are any runes grouped together? Read the runes that fell nearest you first, then work your way towards the furthest side of the circle.

If all the runes fall outside the circle, take it as an indication of that day not being the right time to answer your question and ask again tomorrow!

Multiple Circle Cast

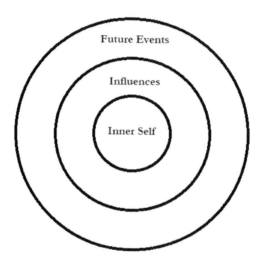

Good for: a general rune reading with more context.

How to do it: draw a large circle on a piece of paper, as with the **Basic Circle Cast,** then draw two circles inside it, roughly even spaced apart.

Next draw three to nine runes from your bag, or muddled pile. Jiggle the runes in your hands while thinking of current issues or clearing your mind entirely, then cast the runes into the circles.

Runes that land in the centre circle align to your inner self, runes that land in the second circle indicate influences that are acting on you or the situation you are enquiring about, runes that land in the outer ring indicate possibly future outcomes. If a rune lands outside all the circles you can either discard it or consider its meaning as something that is on hold for the moment.

You can also adapt the Multiple Circle Cast with your own meanings for each circle. Feel free to experiment and find the casting that works best for you!

Ann J. Clark

End Notes

We hope that you have found this guide a useful start to your adventures in rune divination. If you would like to explore more kinds of divination, take a look at our other books:

Let's try Cartomancy

Let's Try Dowsing

Let's Try Tarot

The Easy Guide to Self-Employment for Tarot Professionals

Ann J. Clark

Bibliography

Arcarti, Kristyna – *Runes for Beginners* (Hodder & Stoughton, 1997)

Blum, Ralph – *The Book of Runes* (Headline, 1993)

Celestine – *Fortune Telling* (Siena, 1998)

Eason, Cassandra – *A Complete Guide to Divination* (Piatkus, 1998)

Eiricksson, Leifur – *The Vinland Sagas* (Penguin Classics, 1997)

Fenton, Sasha - *The Fortune-Teller's Workbook* (The Aquarian Press, 1988)

King, Francis A. – *The Complete Fortune-Teller* (Guild Publishing, 1989)

Larrington, Carolyne. (Trans.) - *The Poetic Edda*, (Oxford World's Classics, 1999)

Tacitus, Mattingly, Harold (trans.) & Rives, James (trans.) – *Agricola and Germania* (Penguin Classics, 2009)

Ann J. Clark

Tyson, Donald – *Rune Dice Divination* (Llewellyn Publications, 1997)

Williams, Athene – "The Runes", in *Fortune Telling* (Marshal Cavendish Books Limited, 1991)

Unknown – *Predicting* (Harper Collins Publishers, 1991)

Online Resources

Newcombe, Rachel – Rune Guide – An Introduction to Using Runes - https://www.holisticshop.co.uk/articles/guide-runes

https://norse-mythology.org/

http://www.therunesite.com/

http://ydalir.ca/norsegods

About the Author

Ann J. Clark is an editor and author in multiple genres of fiction and non-fiction, using multiple author names to keep the collective under control. Her work spans her passions for SFF geekery, history, mythology and visiting ancient sites.

After discovering the tarot and associated divination practices as a teenager, she has read tarot online and in one-to-one environments, co-written tarot courses, and has also run or assisted with various mind/body/spirit trade stalls and online stores.

You can visit her website at
mythmagic.co.uk

Printed in Great Britain
by Amazon

24981634R10056